MW00477954

My Dim Aviary

My Dim Aviary

Gillian Cummings

Black
Lawrence
Press

Black
Lawrence
Press

www.blacklawrence.com

Executive Editor: Diane Goettel
Book and Cover Design: Amy Freels
Cover art: Jean Agélou

Copyright © Gillian Cummings 2016
ISBN: 978-1-62557-958-4

All rights reserved. Except for brief quotations in critical articles or reviews, no part of this book may be reproduced in any manner without prior written permission from the publisher: editors@blacklawrencepress.com

Published 2016 by Black Lawrence Press.
Printed in the United States.

ON HASHISH by Walter Benjamin, translated by Howard Eiland and others, with and introductory essay by Marcus Boon, Copyright © 2006 by the President and Fellows of Harvard College.

Contents

Note   xi

Rêve   1

I.

Rouge   5
Argent   6
Voyeur   7
Toilette   8
Parfum   9
Dentellière   10
Asperges   11
Amie   12
Halo   13
Raisins   14
Odalisque   15
Haschisch   16

II.

Dormant   19
Enfant   20
Gâteaux   21
Altiste   22
Dessin   23
Archet   24
Lettre   25
Cadeau   26
Liaison   27

III.

Disparues 31

Broderie 32

Poupée 33

Cauchemar 34

Burlesque 35

Abeille 36

Musée 37

Haschisch 38

Interdit 39

Opium 40

IV.

Peau 43

Paon 44

Guerre 45

Hiver 46

Dessin 47

Poulain 48

Chaton 49

Chemin de Fer 50

Cauchemar 51

Oiseau 52

Malade 53

Nocturne 57

Notes 59

Acknowledgments 61

For Rich

My Dim Aviary

In smiling, one feels oneself growing small wings. Smiling and fluttering are related…

There arises, quite fleetingly, in a moment of introversion, something like an inclination [words illegible] *to stylize oneself, to stylize one's body…*

—Walter Benjamin, translated by Howard Eiland and others

Note

Who was she? Sometimes referred to now as Miss Fernande, she is thought to have lived in Paris in the early 1900s, modeling for the photographer Jean Agélou, who produced erotic postcards of her image, and possibly— there is a mysterious jail record—working as a prostitute. Some identify her as Fernande Barrey, the wife of Montparnasse artist Léonard Tsuguharu Foujita. Others say she was Fernande Olivier, mistress of Picasso. Neither of these assumptions can be proven. Fernande remains a mystery. And so, for a while, I inhabited her—

Rêve

If you'd be the first darkness, le néant not nothing but pregnant with the little shearwater, the pintail, gannet and grebe. Closed, like this, closed into uttermost opening, opaline blue inside scratchy, black mussel shells. The color of repentance is ashes, but what the color of praise? Answer and I'll give you wind riffling books in a kiosk, roots of heather seeking clouds underground. If you'd be host on my tongue or hosanna, not haste all heat-thickened, spurs or burs burning in the hoarse voice of thicket or bush. If you'd sing. If you'd sing, tuned to turn tears where thorns thumb a ladder up the bare, broken stalk of rose. My swollen hips: wet them once with wonderment, twice with your dry face of salt. Wet them, I mean, only with love, that difficult dream, that dread revelation. Shimmer to river me heavenward. Whisper me softly through sleep. And if a man walk with sea in his shoes and spill them over my pillow of white down, tell him the age of oceans is spelled by a swan taking flight inside the incandescence of streetlamps. And if a man be not wooed by my closed bedroom eyes, give him bread for his barter of lashes and weep. But if a man come with sad eyes like the Christ's, let him know grapes do grow from thorns and figs from thistles drop sweet—

I.

Rouge

What color would God clothe me but red? A crimson cap to keep my head from rain, a carnelian cape to wrap my body in swishy silks of blood-spurt, girl-heat. Who taught me the trail through forest, where to find wood violets limp upon slender stems, how to twine them in wreaths gentler than these hands' caress? It's true: I wanted a warm place, a sight familiar as the bone-home of moon's bed in a cloud-slumbered sky. Truer, still: a stone sang in my stomach—to eat and be eaten. A bite of cherry tart. What animal would God liken me unto, but a wayward sheep, wandering the way of the wolf's spittled growl. And if I found death small as a moss-grown flower, and if the color of my corpse was red as that of my clothes, I would still whisper back to the voice that clambered over me, thick with heat, fur and teeth, this is the way of all loneliness—for only luck comes easy as night birds, to scavenge the unburied heart—

Argent

I awoke to rain. Then the sun's coin slid through a hole in the clouds' pocket—and out rayed the dazzle, more and more, fistfuls and fistfuls of money I took as the leaves take the light. When I came to Paris, this much was urgent: earn your living or starve. All the boys in my village wanted to bed me, so—let my body be my bread, as Jesus' body, baked, breaks to be food of our Communion. What union? Baskets of onions and shallots in the street markets. Chanterelles and mousserons. Saucissons dangling from strings—to look at them—almost obscene, one after another, plumped with pork and salt. I close my eyes when I spread my legs and imagine an old butter churn. The handle thrusting down, but below it: myself a cream thickening, smooth as the sight of a seamless cloudbank, cool and blank. There's a place the soul goes when the body is a field lost to burning. A field of chamomile. Thousands of tiny suns blazing back the one sun's gaze. Scent of honey and hay. Each plush gold pillow a nub to rub. To have become a common whore. Qu'est-ce que j'adore, l'éclat de l'or ou le ternissement de l'argent? Which am I, shine or tarnish? Summer simmering in an autumn pot, these flowers I take as tea early mornings, because at night I can't sleep—and because I can't sleep—

Voyeur

Your body, a horse with distemper, scatters the swallows swerving over a field of mallow, low, low. Gallop to God-speed-you, your nerves race fire, fire blooms poppy-fierce in your face, fire claims the lonely field, also your body, or maybe your soul. Speed! Speed! Nerves catch like sun in calendula, wild tansy, those delicate, determined yellows shaking in wind. Do you want me? How bad? Seems to me, the horse of your body wants to eat all the apples turning to mulch on the orchard floor. Or I name the wrong animal. Is your cock an eager rooster without a harem of hens, a clutch of eggs in the catch—without a house save your dream—without, without—have you knocked on the barn door to hear only the sleep of cows, or stood itching in a patch of nettles, bare to your core from the sore song in your groin? Le cheval, n'est-ce pas? Canter, cantilever, nothing to support you now. A small voice cries no, cries help. Do you want me? Crave is hot, a red star, a giant mouth full of froth, full of rocks: hot, red, round, cinnamon candies to smudge a smear of paint on the tongue—crunched, to crack teeth. You with no face, not even a name, breathing me into the pores of your skin, bleeding me out of your bones. O, la chanson dedans, dedans le pauvre! The sad horse can't constrain its musics, but would, but would try—

Toilette

The world is made of water, that much I can tell. When I look in the mirror, the black lacquer hand mirror I hold, I don't see my face, its nonchalance, its disdain. I see water. Rain on the sidewalk of Passage de Flandre. When it rains, I wonder, can you remember what you have never known? Something sad and clean and pure, like the picture of our city God sees when God sleeps. The cobblestones shine a greyer grey and click with the drops falling as my heels click-clack on the tile floor. I hear what I see: shine of silver sheeting air, a thrumming so quiet the shouts of shopkeepers are a silence. Quand il pleut. Quand quelqu'un pleure. When it cries, the grey sky, les larmes are like the Magdalene's alarm when Jesus revealed his risen body, comme les charmes d'une fille de joie, grown penitent and scared. You can be sad and clean and pure, if you go far enough inside yourself you are against yourself, or under yourself, like the Métro, the train cars tunneling life under life. I owe the water. I owe l'eau something of my soul, the part no one can buy, the better part. To strangers, I'm a body in ribbon-trimmed black stockings, a dress of lace I let fall so my breasts show, a face that gives just enough of lust behind disdain. A face of water. A face of rain. Restez seule, good soul. Keep to what hides you, next to nothing, shimmering, a pour of the pure through air, something of rest and cure and sorrow—

Parfum

So you can guess what I smell like, so you can have more than a glimpse of the girl who won't, though she undresses, unfold herself from the flat paperboard of the card: just so, Jean, the photographer who found me on a street corner in a mess of crumpled crinoline, places on the table as prop a bottle of perfume with an oval atomizer. So you can guess: lilac or rose, gardenia or jasmine. You will guess jasmine, if only for the flower's nocturne, how petals unlock their fragrance when dusk diminishes the light and lays me supine upon your bed-mind under stars. Jasmine, weaving through trellises, wandering the hedges in parks, a name that once meant gift from God. As though, if God could send us something for prayer's answer: this suppleness burnt white, an aroma of milk baths, of plush. The secret feline sting of la chatte. And so that you can pet me, stroke the dark curly hair framing my face: just so, Jean leaves a hairbrush, also on the table. Pour votre imagination. For what you would have of la jolie fille. Your pretty filet. Vous pensez que je suis mignonne, non? If I am not my own, where on this earth will the heavens find me? If I am not here, in this salle de bain, when the moment passes into mist and lifts skyward, where will I linger, pressed to essence like oil?—

Dentellière

Don't tell: draped in mist, I never guessed one day I'd be famous for dressing in less. And what mother would say if she knew, if her eyes hadn't blued from blindness. Year after year she made lace in the style of Alençon. Cap backs and lappets to tidy a lady's hair, a layette for a christening, fine shawls and bridal veils. Her needle looped gossamer into blooms and birds. A saint would float in a tree. A spider at her web, we'd say, and wait for her lace to fall from the pillow it was pinned to, ethereal, constellated, comme une toile des étoiles. To wear mother's lace was to wade in a wash of milk, to bathe in smoothness. To wear her lace: skin caressed by feathers and the breathing bird a swan swimming in pools of swoon. One time it happened, I stole the veil meant for a wealthy patron's wedding. Took it to the woods outside town, the leaves silver with dusk, stuttering in wind, a protestation that ends before it begins. Naked, I wrapped the veil around me. Bride of Christ. Épouse du Christ. Dirty Bride. The devil would take me now—

Asperges

Do you see? If you don't force it, it will come, rising as tender shoots of asparagus rose from their crown of roots in spring, each stiff shaft bearing a purpled tip. Do you see? Mornings, Papa would clip them from their haze of fern, and I, a good girl, never thought twice about growth that spiked through earth—I was a good girl, helped my father rinse spears with ice, pack them in crates for market. Out in groves where plants pried themselves shyly forth in shade, my sister and I listened to warblers trill, got dizzy from their gazouillis, conjured nests from trees that shook with song. At night when he'd take us, first me and then her, upon his lap, we thought nothing except—God's rod and His staff; His seed breeding from the soil each green thing; the asparagus swelling with the season. A good girl. Eating them steamed, with hollandaise. And when I became a bad girl, woe betide me if I looked back on the vagrant vegetable—

Amie

Clotilde found me in the hayloft, sticking straws under my nails. She saw where I'd scratched a broken cross on my wrist where veins sketch a blue delta. And she shrieked, the cuts smeared with blood. Qu'est-ce que tu fais? T'es folle, Fernande! What could I say? I thought, Here. Dig in. Plough the furrow with a heart. Put your mark on me. But she took a kerchief, spit on it and wiped me clean. Ça veut dire quoi? My answer froze to filaments of frost, which came to kill the crops early that year. And when she saw the silence in me settling like drifts of white, she kissed the words I swallowed as snow. First, little bisous all over my cheeks, flakes or flecks of wet. Little bisous until one full baiser on my mouth. I saw a field of stars blinking blue and pink around me, stars such as my mother never stitched, a galaxy of guilt and want. And the place between my legs shivered in one huge surge of wave, the way the wheat bends in a coursing curve of gold when the wind gusts once, fast, against it. T'es folle, Fernande, she said again. And only the horses spoke back to her, with whinnies and tail swishes muffled from below. Only the horses—

Halo

A crown of daisies covers my hair, a wreath of wilting daisies wraps me. Petals crooked, warped like thorns. I look up. My chin, lifted. My mouth closed firm as if I keep a secret shared with God. As if, no matter what, He will say of my body, flesh of His flesh. You can see my breasts in this photo, the aureoles of my nipples. You can see two beauty marks on my face, one above my lip, one high on my cheek, made from black eye pencil. I think that here I'm the Magdalene. But Jesus has said my seven demons can stay mine. Mine to be smudged with like a stranger's words: cocotte, connasse, gourgandine, grue, poule, poufiasse, putain. Mine the way les marronniers dans le Jardin du Luxembourg drop their chestnuts with a crack, and the soft shell splits to let the hard kernel out, shiny and ready to be squirreled into ground. God the Father splits me like this, for my soul sometimes can't find my body. And Jean splits me from my image, the girl with chestnut brown hair from the girl all sepia shades—

Raisins

Jean didn't want to show me with a glass of wine. He thought the grapes
themselves more sensual. Provocative. Thick clusters of fruit ripening
on gnarled ropes of vine, a September sky ghosting the morning's hills
with fog. Sauvignon. Chenin Blanc. Muscadelle. Semillon. An aroma of
melon, cinnamon, acacia—or linden blended with lemon and honey.
We guessed: which tang on the tongue would tempt you? So he said,
You want those grapes like you want a man with money and a big cock,
your raison d'être. And I thought: the Eucharist. I want these grapes the
way the disciples wanted to swallow Christ's soul. Whole and round
and ripe. The grapes' terroir, my terror. The seeds sunken inside, Jesus'
judgment on the hard bite of my temper, opposite of these too tender
teeth. So I draped the grapes over my open mouth, as if all the world
could be eaten—

Odalisque

My Pasha, I picture you in yellow silk, like a woman's, your robe untied, undone—the sash slack at your waist, the sea of yellow parting and the red fish, the sprightly red fish alone in its body of water, leaping for luck, rising out of its element, its tides and brine—to be caught, as I am caught by the camera. I can only pose if I picture you this way, vulnerable, as a fish is vulnerable to the hook, as a sea is vulnerable to the storms God sends, darkening and quickening the waves. What surges in you? What crests and foams and churns? M'avez-vous choisi? The way the light chooses me, raying from a high window, all artifice of paint. I sit on a patterned pillow, crafted of coarse wool. It chafes, but I sit still for you. Draped beneath me, a Persian carpet unscrolls in arabesques— the shapes remind me of the leaves this time of year, each singular in its burning, yellow or red, living its last gasp more perfectly in a parallel realm, where elm and maple sear the air with color, yet remain whole outside time. In heaven, all remains unbroken like this vase that curves as my hips curve into my waist, as your unbroken gaze stays steady upon me, following the lilt in the lift of my arm, bangled with serpentine coils that would turn tongue and hiss, Temptress, Temptress, if copper could voice its vice. Big fish, little fish, you take the bait, Monsieur, but I'm the one with gills, killed by the click of the aperture—

Haschisch

And it's the wind—an afternoon no one wanted me, I climbed the stepped streets from Pigalle up Montmartre and sat down on a cold stone ledge. My décolleté dress turned drafty: I clung to my thin, fringed shawl the way a child wraps in wool, trying to hide from the dark inside the day. The sun pushed hard, but it couldn't do a thing against the wind—it's the wind that comes to mind when Jean says, Sleep the sleep of ivresse, the rush of trance, the drug in your veins like the shadow of a stranger wooing you without form. When he poses me, hand over head in a spell of faint, my body soft-sprawled on the carpet beside the hookah—it's the wind that comes back: how a flock of pigeons swarmed then scattered then swarmed together again, shifting one to one to one on the wind's pivot, blown through sky, a cloud of flap and glide, a storm of gesture. How the birds winged the same spirals as the leaves, the leaves that beneath them funneled in a whirl to match their flying, the crisped, curled leaves of October's dying. And it was the leaves that said, I am no more, I am no more, even as they shifted with a crinkle sort of sound. The leaves that were and weren't. The doves quickly gone from sight—the same doves in the Kingdom of Heaven? If the drug rushes, this is the rush of it. Jean behind his camera, me in your eye. We are here now, here now, here now—and gone—

II.

Dormant

I didn't know of the fairy's curse. I was a girl of quenched fires, wanted little. But a spool of wool, to have it whole in my hands, to spin it thin as the wind's hair: how my soul sought sheep beyond counting. This is how I slept once I'd fingered the spindle, as if so deep in a cave nothing could remind me of black. As if starless skies over the fold and the flock voiceless, bleating silence unto the shepherd of their slaughter. Everyone who sleeps is meek, even the executioner, if dreams don't come. I lay unconscious, sprawled on my back like a broken doll, my face a moon over acres of thorn. Vines snarled the birches, their bark peeled like skin. This I knew later, according to him, the prince who with a kiss said softly, Bloom, Briar Rose. Then the colors rushed in, the reds of the curtains, the faint blue beyond like a trace of where I'd been.... Then the colors rushed out, when Maman told me this story at bedtime, my body folding inward as if to bury clouds of fleece—

Enfant

Warm and soft. I'm inside the warm and soft. Mother's hand is moving over me in smooth after smooth. It's a round feeling. It's a yawn of falling inside. Mother's hand has a rhythm like rocking. I don't know what goes up and down and what presses, only it's warm. Mother makes a breeze in my nose. The breeze is sweet and heavy. I want more. I want it, but it comes and goes, like her hand. All of this is to say I remember how mother untied my bonnet, stroked my hair, how she tucked a lavender heart pillow where I lay my head. Only later could I say, This happened. Only after we cut long stalks, tied them to rafters to dry upside-down, crushed flowers from stems with a rolling pin to fill sachets with the scent of sleeping. One day, stitching lace to heart's rim, I had a moment of Oh!: mother's touch, the lull and lure of drowse, me so little in the cradle I couldn't know the strange smell's source. And if I saw something as a baby, it was the same as the singing inside. And if I heard singing, it was as one hears in a dream, a song from faraway, a surge of tides, warm water washing the dreamer the way dusk dims the purple gardens glazing the hills. Mother, lover, teach me to bathe like this—

Gâteaux

Have you once known the sweetness of God's true name whispered as your own? As though to call your soul outward to the borders of your body and beyond? Like that, he whispered a name, not Fernande, in my ear—a name of his making, too secret to tell. As we lay together in my room at the Hôtel Franche-Comté, he placed his hands down the length of me, softly sweeping my skin to the susurration of these syllables, not to make me his but to make me more mine. The room dark. I could barely see his expression. His name, what I should call him, as unknown to me as an unborn foal is mystery, swelling the body of the mare. But I could feel the cold band of his ring. And because I didn't want to feel cheap, I took the money. Took it and bought beaucoup de pâtisseries: un éclair, un millefeuille, un chausson aux pommes, until finally l'opéra. This last one, one thin layer over another: the soft joconde nutty from almonds, the slightly bitter chocolate ganache, coffee buttercream like a mouthful of cloud, layer over layer smooth and horizontal as some call the more refined women of my kind: les grandes horizontales. I've never been to the opera, never heard singing that rings like the voices of angels. But on that night I knew sweetness as touch, as sound. So the pastries: I ate them for God-knows-what-reason, maybe revenge against my body's giving, to force it to take more of what it loves, more and still more, to take and take—

Altiste

Don't touch me so tenderly this time, I tell him. He points to the case in the corner, curved hips to waist to bust, the viola hidden behind locks, silver closures snapped shut. I can be rough with her too, he says. When I hurt her, she cries most plaintively, her voice filled with awe at her ache. He makes me think of how flesh longs for a lashing, the way love must be love if it burns. Hand over hand, we pull off the buttons of his shirt, snapping thread. Avec tes dents, he says. I bite like scissors. Then scratch his back in slow strokes that leave pink stripes. When he turns over, do I lower my mouth? He waves no, touches my cheek, like so, as a petal falls upon moss, almost weightless. I could kill him for such sadness. Our Lord in the garden of Gethsemane bore his grief with a cup of light, steeled his sorrow to a shimmer, pearl grey as the coming dawn. My body violable as the carved instrument in its case of wood and leather. The violist knows this with each taut horsehair of his bow. And the viola knows the echo of pain is the silence of the world within the soul—

Dessin

Dusk light, early, shuts us in. On the floor, sheets of paper thin as the silk I'm not wearing. Lie down flat, he says, in a tone I can't crack, his command neither cold nor soft but bending like a sapling in a place of too much wind—that sore, green spike, that seize of need. I do as I'm told, my eyes fixing the ceiling for fear they'll fix his. He touches the top of my head with a pencil. A tickle down my cheek, down my neck, as the edge of me, where I disappear into everything else, is claimed as real, a tickle more like hackles as if to join body to world with a line is dangerous—or to separate. The pencil moves the length of my leg, around my foot, five bumps for toes, and up. It grazes my inner thigh, and I think, Oh, but he will not! L'altiste n'est pas si méchant! Tease, he touches me over and over, blunt stick rubbing a knot of lines into paper, a nest woven of my want. He desires my desire, that it should never abate, and should never be matched by his. Only this man, only this one, who could take me as easily as the soldiers took Jesus, never a meeker, more submissive subject, only this man from whom I would accept even a sprig of mint, an anise seed—Stand, he says, paint yourself in. I can't, don't want to, yet I do. Yellow-green for my head, for the skin of an onion, thoughts within thoughts within thoughts whittled to nothing but the too-easy tears of a girl given onions for love—

Archet

If a fly lands on a horse, the horse's flesh will quiver, a ripple-flash of instinct firing the supple muscles; its tail will twitch, whipping air with hairs long as the wind's white voice. If wind swells full of water, a pine will let lodge in its capillaries the sticky caulk of sap, tapped amber when resin-thieves come to bleed the tree. And the horse and the humble fly, the wind breaking to rain and the green-needled spirit of stillness, all these bend into sound when the world is poured through by music. This is how he plays my body, how he rosins his bow with pine and gold, tightens the tension to taut, how he scrapes the slick horsehairs over my skin to call forth my trembles and moans. Vibrato. His bow against my thighs. The way the strings snap back in place, hundreds of times per second with each draw, the way he ushers an auster, a bluster of thunder. This warm rain tingling, it pings the green needles, its drops collect, they fall like a loosening, like a foal's first chance to wander. Soft, a whisper, tremolo, gathering to gallop, faster and fast—When I search his face, his eyes are closed, as though to hear in our duet one song, or to blind himself to the wounds he's wrought. And the music in the room quiets to the catch of my breath, to his awe at my waking as his instrument would wake, taken from the dark of its case, reminded of pasture and forest—

Lettre

Lose yourself but lose yourself backwards. Leave your life by allowing the small death to happen, the leap in dark lake, clean water closing its lilies, its turtles, the slugs of its mud. The soul you would lift in sleepless coils, lilting like larks towards a cloud-clamored sun, let it come down, let it sink, listless, lackadaisical, its dropped pebble dopplering rings in the ratio of ripples' surrender. Lâchez-vous, lâchez tout. Let the soul drown, swallowed by the body. Rest, lean your length on the column of fortune's flattery, lean and lounge as I've learned: let the silver slabs of stone you balance on be ballast to your ballet, be throne to your body's lithe latitudes, sleek as minks licking the spill of their fur. Lean and let go. Lentement, lentement. And then, lourde mais liesse, a weight with wings, laugh, laugh a little, smile as though you'd fly, shoulders fledged, arms upon the air, your fingers tapered, delicate as flames of feather, your hands candling calls to the lost listener who bends an ear to the silence of your form. Mon âme, mon élève, laissez le meilleur pour la fin. Lose yourself to the lure of light's pure pilgrimage as it claims a temple of your skin, and you and all you've held to in your life proven its relic, its icon, its holy thing brillianced in the center of its shrine, your flesh finally hallowed, full and whole, poured out upon the world like molten gold. Lower yourself, humbled, into the calm of this still light, your home in the body like a letter folded backwards, enveloped, couched in the lap of the Lord—

Cadeau

It is quiet, so quiet, the snow cries in the street with no sound. It is cold, so cold, the air a frozen river calling the soul to drown. Oh, but it is Noël, past midnight. Christ came clean of Mary's blood and curled in the crèche like a cabbage, each leaf of his life to be unpeeled down to light. There is a gulf at the center, a gaping wound. The chiming bells have stopped, the voices of carolers who chose warm beds over chill. Priez pour nous. This is what he gives me when he comes to my door under dark of the one star. I untie the neat bow, let the ribbon fall. Inside: a necklace, thin string of gold draping a saint's pendant: Marie-Madeleine, priez pour nous. This is what I am or should be: his penitent. I let him piece the clasp together behind my neck and something breaks. I think of myself in Jean's studio, the peek-a-boo pose where a bouquet freights my lap. How I fold my palms together, almost in prayer, and hold them under my bowed head, my eyes raised, not at the camera, not at anything—at the thought of love, which for me wasn't anything. In the room with this man, my eyes well. Sainte Marie-Madeleine, priez pour nous. He calls me his swan. There is a swan gouging its breast with its bill. The lakes of France are frozen. Where do swans swim, gracing the star-shimmered waters with their impossible bodies, their hearts too fierce to falter?—

Liaison

The moment he took my body to his, the world was water. I heard rain, rain on the sidewalk of Passage de Flandre, rain on the boulevards, rain on the tin roofs, a thrumming so hard it could only be made of softness. I saw trees slick, bare and black in the showers sheeting the city. And one tree I saw clearly, a silhouette of elm. One branch, one twig, I saw. How a drop of water clung and in its orb a shine, as from a streetlamp. How a second drop fell on the first, and together they swelled so full they quivered—it was all they could do not to break, to hold on. And heavy, too heavy to bear their union, they fell to the sidewalk beneath the tree, not knowing what became of themselves—

III.

Disparues

The missing among us, the vanished girls, speak as damp shadows under stones, cool and mossy and still, a silence like God's. A key, a small key, forbidden to use, keeps the chill of blood in the cellar, a stain that won't rub off with sand or pumice or the frenzy of hands to hide what the body knows: heavy hang the apples engorged on broken boughs. I called to my sister, Let your vision be our prayer, let horses trample earth hot with speed to cancel this fever gonging soundless in our temples. Yet all she could say from her vantage is there's dust in the sun and green in the ignorant grass—my throat beneath the knife. I would tell her I've learned a silken tapestry, a golden goblet, the perfect mirrors are murder. Show me a woman who doesn't seek death and I'll close a door that never opened. Show me a man whose beard isn't blue—I can't even point at the sky—

Broderie

The sky is doing this. Or is the earth calling for embroidery and an answer is silver threading air quicker than a million seamstress' hands? The earth hot for needles, roofs ringing thimbles, empty of stubbed thumbs. God is crewel, freely stitched, or prick and pounce. His wide eyes swallow all the brothels of this city, all the girls alone in their rooms, mending time with what they can't cry into cloth. The girls would drown boats of bread foundered in fondue, if only to call the toasted cheese at bottom la religieuse. Quiet when the rain ends, when the storm snaps its strings. Something once habitual has no home, no bed. What unravels might unravel—

Poupée

I tell myself, Fernande, quit your girly girl act. But in my chest is a child and in the child a doll, a porcelain doll I never owned. She is of two minds and each eye spies a sky that would make the other shudder: red night for the princess locked like a lunatic in a ward of whores, white day neat as daisies for the witch who'd brew a slew of warts to speckle a bad trick's balls. Either way, her hands fall off, broken at the wrists. Either way, a pimp pins her up as his puppet, and she flails her arms as if sweeping dead flies from the sky. I had a real doll and gave her to my sister. My sister planted her in the dirt. To grow more dolls. Now in my village, all the girls have tin eyes and bat their lashes at the belfry. Sometimes, I don't want this. I don't want bells to peal as if the soul's a seduction. I don't want rings of reverberation to snare my sister in her dreams. And yet girls will preen and strut. And spider cracks run. Quand la cloche sonne—

Cauchemar

Everything is loud and shaking. I'm being pummeled by pomegranates. One hit would hurt enough, but the plunder of sky's store leaves me pelted, a skinned chamois. The fruits fall, a disastrous rain from barn-red clouds, lowing unabated. Bruise crowds the boulevards and arcades, scanning for someone to strike a deal with pain. Loud and shaking. Gamblers bet on baccarat, every card a queen red with juice. I bite my lip for salt and taste sour-sweet seeds I spit square as teeth. The fruits burn like conscience. Sin! Sin! It's hard to be a soft thing when rain grows rinds, when wind hammers its snares and cymbals, rendering me mute—

Burlesque

Early September. Sun hot on rocks of the stony field, hot on the quivering wheat. Breath of boys in the classroom: a mirage of chalk dust. Bless them as they waited without knowing. We would come to them plumed and silky, birds of the Orient, an oasis of tease. Clotilde and I cut school to dress in stolen costumes: she in black bolero jangling coins over scarlet satin, me in fleshings stitched with spirals of pearl to cover my oyster-shell breasts, my near-bare pubis, a cape fashioned of peacock feathers to drape the last hue of dusk over pale dunes. Bless the boys lost in their books, their sexes swathed in knickers. We'd hide behind a woodpile, smoking, until they filed out, all scuffle and din, and Clotilde would kick her leg high, I'd let fall the scandal of my sheath. The boys speechless as sand until laughter monsooned over them. Dieu bénisse tes pénises, we'd proclaim, tripping, running, as the headmaster shouted his threats. And then we'd stop, turn, and Clotilde would warn him: Pope Sixtus the Fourth built a brothel and fashioned himself a fortunate pimp—

Abeille

Obey the nun-queen in her waxen abbey, obey the dew-drunken drone. Amber is the color of ache, and my sister ate her insides empty of nectar's plenty. She was a good bee. She puked her food in a bucket and buried the waste in the woods. Her hunger, her honey, she sang sylvanly, sweetly, in the children's choir, abuzz with a beauty that brims in the voice when the body hears the silence of its bones. Summers, she gathered poppies, bachelor's buttons and blue gentian under skies heavy with crows. Even air could weight her legs like scopa packed with pollen, even wind scourge her skin to warn the soul it's not free of fat's toll. Maigre, sa silhouette. Meager, my answer: eager to leave her, so I wouldn't have to see. Mélisse felt father's eyes upon her. I knew this when I left. He puffed his pipe and smoked her from her hideout in the hive, while mother hurried to hoard nourriture for her sick bee to heave. Obey heaven, obey the burn of the dying sun. Comment elle a volé de ce qu'elle ne voulait pas. But a bee can only beat its wings for so long—

Musée

Because the Mona Lisa is gone now, stolen by night and the secrets of night. Because they could have stared at her long and slow, these strangers, as they stare at me from beneath their hats, here on the steps to the Louvre where a widow holds bread in her hands, winged by pigeons who take her stooped shoulders as perch, where a small girl follows, tottering, to spook birds skyward, torn dress, scuffled shoes, but a face that glows the way La Joconde's did, like a question posed by the moon, sfumato soft, a peach to cup, ashy at the edges. Because every woman is mystery, ruined. Because a woman won't stay bound in body alone, wrapped round in cloth, a Victoire, with wings to stretch into cloud, her heart empty as our thoughts of one another, as their question, Combien? and my answer, Je ne dis que oui. Because the old woman spills her sack of crumbs and comes closer, fledged for borrowed flight. Because the child frowns and skulks. Because what remains is nowhere and is now—

Haschisch

Persian carpet again, as it was years ago. Same patterned pillow of wool. Moroccan vase marked with a geometry of green and gold leaves, its swelled bowl at bottom graciling gourd-like to its long, thin neck. Same rusty hookah as prop. To come here to pose after three men at once upon me. Knowing nothing but billows of blue, my knees against bear fur and prods in every orifice, my sex slackening to pained sleep from the flood of it, de trop. To feel the fur that was beneath me knifed from the animal, its head still attached to its hide, the open mouth arced in an anguish too large for its teeth. Disheveled, smelling of musk and cum, to come here through the market at Les Halles, suckling pigs swinging on hooks at the butchers' stands, skinned rabbits with their soft, amazed eyes, as if flayed alive. Now to be shackled in slave bangles, to see Jean changing the plates with each exposure—to be exposed, inside outside, blood flushing my flesh. And Jean wants me to smile of all things—

Interdit

From the back of the barn, where he took me in hay scent and odor of manure, I could almost see the church spire, the cross wired on the sky like the brand of man on the mystery, a pivot of history to swirl the commotion of constellations and clouds. Was it freedom from netting or a winged thing's capture? Was it a death or the quiet that comes after? This is how Papa told me he loved me, unbuckled and unbridled, how I answered back with hushed restraint, fire licking the lengths of my legs as they blushed, loose with the danger of this thing we did. I can only find it here now, lost in some closet like an old Bible pressing feathers of swallows and shrikes, binoculars beside. It comes when I pass ponies chewing from buckets, or worse, ponies with children astride their curry-combed backs. It comes, for a moment, when I first put on black, as if a seduction will kill—and the loss be small as the child's red lollipop, and the loss be invisible as the animal's panted breaths—

Opium

The truth I know would be the field and not the sky, the manyness of grasses bearing the weight of wind. No one will say it, but the sky is heavy, its silence a clamor like the ether of lead. The lack I love is a single stalk of poppy, holding alone all the webs spiders spin in their sorrows, brazen enough to raze the field in a flare, one gust of color, wrinkled tissue, one tassel to tussle the long, broad boredoms of this broken land. The poppy, demimondaine, denizen bedizened, the poppy, blowsy and drowsed, cupping the drowned candles of the rain. And the rain. Come the rain, come in thousands, come rest and merge, meld into the spill of eros the poppy bleeds into earth—

IV.

Peau

Kill someone, said the voice of the forest. I could ask my father to kill the donkey with ears soft as pussywillows, whose manure fell to earth as tithings of gold. I was a girl but I could do this, myself dead three times in dresses shimmering silver as stars, orb-white as the moon, the last a yellow burn like sun at dawn, all blaze to blare the blur of my father into sharpened sense. But his lust was a rock smoothed by water, and what was hard in him called for hands like the river's, my own hands cradling a cup of hyssop to spasm my spine into shivers. I never saw the henchmen slay the donkey, but I stole its grey skin and ran. Muddied my face with silt, hid in the hide smelling of misfortune, a wretchedness that told I was wrecked. When you've been dead, stars prick your skin with the tiniest logic. The moon gives light in darkness. The sun gives light in light. When an old kitchen maid took me in to scrape ovens clean of char, I knew but this: hope is a gold ring, an empty circle, something waiting to be filled. You can bake it in a prince's cake, but sift the flour finely—

Paon

Jean seats me before a backdrop of somber skies. At my feet, roses and leaves crimped as the life that summered inside them dies to its fires. Jean won't say it, but I know what I know: we haven't many sessions left together. Years ago, always the tender blooms, la douceur. Now the singe-smell of earth returning to earth. Behind me, painted as sentinel to the storm, a peacock stands waiting for rain. Vanity of vanities—but what of this moment? The iridescence of its train, aquamarine and turquoise, emerald, viridian and lime, a hundred eyes by which to see God, or which God, in his mild mercy, sees. Scrape the quills across my skin. Chasten me, if you would. Corrigez-moi. I believe in this bird that can fly only to its roost, damaged by decadence. The storms of heaven extinguish stars, and the peacock shrieks a deafening cry—

Guerre

When glaziers removed the windows from Sainte-Chapelle and strangers no longer knelt, palms pressed together, their bodies still as the blue vault above. When butterflies no longer fluttered the fractured air in blues, reds, yellows, papillons of prayer, spoken for ghosts of the not-yet-unremembered. When sirens shook the city to warn the sky might soon break as easily as stained glass circles of saints—then he returned to me. When he was not unafraid—

Hiver

Je mange du pain. Ce n'est pas la peine. Winter sifts snow like flour into the bowl of earth. Horses' hooves knead it to dough. I eat bread like pain, little else available, and wrap in woolens moths once made their own. In place of music, rations of coal; in the Opéra, where he unwound scarves of sound, his dark silk, now crowds of hands clamor for a last piece of heat, myself a small hunger, a shiver among the throng. It won't last long. Will knell till Judgment. The newspapers, morning and evening, spell death tolls from the front. He hasn't gone but waits. I tell him not to speak. He says white is his favorite color. Sacré Coeur, now completed, bleeds white when it rains, as though stones cry the color of sorrow. Sorrow because it blinds, this hurt, like knowing God and having to leave Him. Now snow falls on sidewalks, in trenches, over meadows where mines burrow with moles. The snow-light opaline at dawn, shimmering, as if so many souls lost allow the sky its glow—

Dessin

The faces in crowds, I draw them. The old woman with eyes wide as moons on lake water, wrinkles around like ripples to worry the light: this woman looked at me with the honesty of shadows and I saw the mesh bag of tomatoes she hauled as the night sky hefts our dreams, and suddenly tomatoes were water and sky, a face round, red and laden with hopes too sorry not to carry. . . . A boy alone with a ball, a small boy with the look of having known too much absence: he tossed his ball against brick and even the brick turned him away, giving back and giving back only the echo of a smack to remind him. . . . The faces of strangers, I sketch them, to make them stay. Because I know they end where I end, in the image on paper, the grey outline, smoke that turns to water and rains on the future's mind. Because we are all ink in the dark and charcoal in night's stove. . . . But by day, their faces are like light on water: a glint and each visage vanishes, back to blue, yet face after face, they play radiance over the depths, the shallows. I see the Seine in sun, peopled by light. The sparks signal souls made whole for an instant by the meeting of river and sky: we are alive this way, blood and breath, and when we die we end in the glimmer that precedes us and follows. . . . I draw them, the strangers, for something to connect us, rubber balls and tomatoes, for something to remain—

Poulain

Morning entered the room like fog. My arm around his waist as he slept: the softness of his skin, the softness of the light: a foal stepping, tentative, on legs long as meadow grass, wobbly, to be something so fragile begotten in a hard world. This innocence in him, this goodness. Bon in the marrow and marrow in the bone. Brome and wild oat, the breath of the animal swelling its sides, tremor and twitch. I told him of the baby, how it was not his, how I would take care of it. How he could leave if he had to, steal across the field where winds are wounds, unsure how to hide in the light, his body built nimble but not for this—

Chaton

Maybe in what you cannot forgive, a small space opens, like the first glimpse of blue when clouds break after weeks of rain. So I have come to think of my father. When Clotilde's cat gave birth to kittens, I loved the little black one, a slinky sylph of a thing, fur that purred the silk of night, eyes blinking a cosmos through a blurring hue, chatoyant. Such trusting eyes. When I sat with my parents and sister at déjeuner and asked, my mother said no. She thought a black cat would bring bad luck. It was my father who said, Let the girl have her kitten. She has brought us enough bad luck already. And in his voice no anger, but a kind of remorse or supplication—

Chemin de Fer

Everything's going away. The sad hush of rain dims the echo of a child on the platform, calling, calling her dog, her voice high and thin as the small wailing of mosquitoes swarming the marsh places, now empty of heat. Through runnels streaming the window, I see Clotilde, her face inside my reflection, thrown back by the ambient light: we were part of each other, we were inside each other, we doubled together as one ghost. How does the soul leave the body and the body go on, forgetting.... The man in the grey coat who turned to give us a sudden, concentrated look when we embraced, embarrassed by the thin crowd descending, embarking, hurriedly in the rain—this man's gaze portends no good. I see Clotilde waving, waving, inside the apple of my face, her hand around a kerchief to keepsake a meteor shower of lost days. It's as if the dead came here to haunt us, to say, On fera des voyages de silence. You'll be alone, finding each other in stranger's arms, alone in the rain that burns you, wet in the way of fire, soft in the way of iron—

Cauchemar

Nuns pass over snow like a flock of crows descended. The silence of crows is a cane's lash. I go where the nuns won't find me: into a greenhouse that bears the name Bottle of Worldly Sorrows. The plants grow thick. Palms and vines. Orchids with a hiss of hot throat. The light blue-green and misty. A girl appears. She is so small it's hard to believe she can talk. I will die here, she says, unless you save me. A needle pings against glass. The greenhouse gives, shattered panes shocking the lush leaves with slice and snow-air. I hold the girl in my arms and run. Fecund green collapses under sheets of ice. We hear the words, Nowhere is near enough to heaven. And again: Nowhere. Nulle part—

Oiseau

Numbly, the body owns its cold. This morning I watched pigeons and sparrows peck the crust of ice, what the odd snowfall left, a scattering of safflower seeds and dried corn, watched their shadows hover over snow, blue shadows teaching the white not to blind. Ombres des ailes: sometimes my ailment moves like them, ténébreuse, double. A little bird, unbroken, palpitates where it fell. How do you kill what struggles, a pulse at its throat like a plea? Tomorrow will die here, all no to my rusty drum, my dim aviary, the cage of my womb. It's not about a place of cold music, shrill calls to shut coos. It's not how pennyroyal steams the dawn. Pigeons sleep not knowing the ledge ends and wake to rose light too soft for this season. When the dark bird lands upon the horse's back, it kicks open, the most innocent horse, the death horse, drowsed, white—

Malade

I keep to my bed, hot with a fever born of hemorrhage. If the rooftops and sidewalks, if the horse-carts and blanketed horses, the automobiles that put our strongest geldings to shame—if all of Paris, weighted under layerings of the cold stars heaven sends to remind earth of a harsher purity—A knock on the door. Pas maintenant, s'il vous plaît. But it is he, the only man I would let in, the quiet man, the man with the viola. He asks nothing of me, as the snow asks nothing. He brings a bucket by the bed, lays a cold cloth on my head. Waits while I drift in dreams true to neither sleep nor waking, of angels glittering the threshold with crystal facets of their weird beauty. In the angels' world, no one wears— each one is: a negligee of neige, a powder peignoir. Or so I see. Or think I am. I don't know the last time I ate anything. I don't know if my body will desire any kind of entering again. When the man turns to leave, he tucks a flower in my hand, the bloom of a hothouse waxplant: one perfect cluster of white, pink and maroon stars within stars, each star five-pointed and seeming to spin as the real stars spin and flame out of unrest or love, you never know which till you dissolve, as they do, come dawn, over the shivering city—

Nocturne

A plea for this moment of water's no color, no taste, that is midnight over mud-leaf brown, that is bitten fish seepage borrowed from the sky under sky. We are alone inside the moan and cry of music, where moon sheds its shine on a loneliness lost, forever ours inside the swan of our bodies' glister and glide, where he leans into what carries us, what feathers us forth. If I hold to one note in song's unscrolling, I wound the swan's legs with a stone dragging lake bottom. If beauty becomes unbearable, then there's ruin for the world's welter of white: the pear orchard to unpetal in the swan's clouded slumber, a blossom's fragrance bedded deep inside fruit-meat of the fast-beating heart. Better to let music live as wings on water, something impossibly here, how sky meets and mounts its mirror of echoing underflow, the way our bodies melt to shine and shadow-flight: one bird born to the weight of darkness, wrecked by light rapturing each shingle of spine, each nexus of nerve. Diminuendo. Nothing is diminished when air carries bone—

Notes

Disclaimer: While Fernande and Jean Agélou were real persons, all of the scenes described herein are entirely the work of the author's imagination.

"Archet:" The phrase, "the way the strings snap back in place, hundreds of times per second with each draw" was borrowed, almost verbatim, from a website that has since been changed: http://www.ehow.com/about_5414858_types-violin-rosin.html.

"Musée:" The *Mona Lisa* was stolen from the Louvre in August 1911. It would take two years before the painting was found and returned.

"Chemin de Fer:" I owe this poem to the help of Vijay Seshadri who provided phrases as writing prompts. These phrases became the scaffolding of the poem.

Sources for information on Miss Fernande include: Christian Bourdon's *Jean Agélou: de l'académisme à la photographie de charme*, Ferrucio Farina's *Venus Unveiled* and Louis La Volpe's *Miss Fernande: First Lady of Erotica*, as well as the website: http://missfernande.com/.

Acknowledgments

Thank you to the kind editors of the following journals, in which some of these poems first appeared, sometimes in earlier versions:

The 2River View: "Halo" and "Raisins"
Boulevard: "Dormant"
BOXCAR Poetry Review: "Lettre"
CALYX Journal: "Interdit"
Colorado Review: "Disparues" and "Rouge"
Crab Orchard Review: "Dentellière"
The Cream City Review: "Oiseau"
Denver Quarterly: "Argent," "Haschisch (And it's the wind),"
    "Opium," "Toilette" and "Voyeur" (as "Équine")
Front Porch Journal: "Poupée"
The Laurel Review: "Dessin (The faces in crowds, I draw them)" and
    "Rêve"
The Massachusetts Review: "Peau"
PANK: "Amie" and "Chemin de Fer"
The Paris-American: "Nocturne"
Requited Journal: "Asperges" and "Enfant"
Sister Ignition: "Altiste," "Archet," "Dessin (Dusk light, early, shuts us
    in)" and "Gâteaux"

"Liaison" was first published in the anthology *Myrrh, Mothwing, Smoke: Erotic Poems* (Tupelo Press, 2013).

Great gratitude to Diane Goettel and the editors and staff of Black Lawrence Press: thank you for making this book real!

Thank you to my family, friends and teachers for the support you offered during the writing of this book. Nan Becker, Kate Knapp Johnson,

Claudia Cortese, Traci Brimhall, Eugenie Juliet Theall, Jennifer Franklin, Dave Gelfand and Martha Rhodes: I needed your help with this manuscript and you were generous in your critiques and encouragement. Gallia Taranto, thank you for reading over an early manuscript and correcting the errors in my French. Tomoko Yagi, thank you for your friendship and for sharing with me your enthusiasm in reading. I don't think this book would exist if you hadn't told me to read Allison Benis White's *Self-Portrait with Crayon*. To Pam Hart: the title you magically pulled out of the air was the best title I could have imagined—thank you for that and for your thoughtful reading and reordering of the manuscript when it needed much help.

Thank you to the mysterious Fernande, who became my muse for this series of poems. I hope I have not harmed the memory of you in my reimagining of a story that could have been yours. And thank you to Jean Agélou for the photographs, without which I would have had no reason to write.

Finally, endless and unfathomable love beyond love for Rich Panish. I wrote this book for you.

Photo: Rich Panish

My Dim Aviary is Gillian Cummings' first book. She has also written three chapbooks, *Ophelia* (dancing girl press, 2016), *Petals as an Offering in Darkness* (Finishing Line Press, 2014), and *Spirits of the Humid Cloud* (dancing girl press, 2012). Her poems have appeared in *Barrow Street, Boulevard, The Cincinnati Review*, the *Colorado Review, The Cream City Review, Denver Quarterly, The Laurel Review, Linebreak, The Massachusetts Review, The Paris-American, Quarterly West,* in other journals and in the anthologies *Myrrh, Mothwing, Smoke* (Tupelo Press, 2013) and *The Doll Collection* (Terrapin Books, 2016). In 2008, she was awarded a Dorothy Sargent Memorial Fund Poetry Prize. A graduate of Stony Brook University (BA, English) and of Sarah Lawrence College's MFA program, Gillian lives in Westchester County, New York. She is also a visual artist.